CULTURE CHANGE AMONG THE NAGA TRIBES OF MYANMAR

The former headhunters seek to modernize

by **OLK BON**

olkbon@gmail.com

March, 2019

1. Methodology

In January 2019, the author of the study interviewed several tribe members, by visiting the townships of

1)   Layshi [or Leshi, names of the tribes: Jejara or Para, Makuri (Chera village), Dan Gion, Long Phuri (Yobami village), Tangkhul (Ngachan village)].

2)   Hkamti [or Zingaling Khamti, names of the tribes: Hai Mi (Aung Mye Village), Khiamniungam (Tsomniu village)],

3)   Lahe [Chamchang subtribe of Tang Shen, Chan subtribe of Konyak tribe (Yinchong village), Lainong tribe (Longchem Nokgong village)].

4)   In addition, he had the opportunity to meet the Naga people that came from Nanyun (or Namyung) township (tribe of Tang Shen, previously called Pangmi or Hai Mi) and the Nagas of India (the Chakhesang and Phokungri tribes).

2. Abstract

The research involves an analysis of the Naga culture, type of cultural change and comparison with other tribes. It answers how the changes impact the culture and life, which leads to an explanation of the culture change.

The author's choice of focusing on the Nagas of Myanmar (Eastern Nagas) was due to the fact that the research on these hill tribes is limited in comparison to the Nagas of India (Western Nagas). He also wanted to note the developments in the face of the democratization of Myanmar. This paper aims to contribute toward identifying the problems of community, by offering the first-hand info. The delimitation of the study comes from the fact that culture is large and complex, and it is impossible to be studied as a whole.

*(1) Photo below: The Naga Hills lie on the bor-
der of India and Myanmar.*

3. Background

The Naga tribes have lived for centuries in the northwestern corner of what is now called the Union of Myanmar and face challenges. With admiration, they look at their relatives from Nagaland, the part of democratic India, comparing their levels of education, healthcare and road quality. The partly democratic political system of Myanmar, with the military holding a grip over the government, brings some hope even to this tiny community. The Nagas reveal the problems faced by all minority groups in this repressive country.

4. Question of the Naga Zone

The Naga Self-Administrated Zone (or Naga Zone) in the current shape emerged in the aftermath of the changes made to the Myanmar constitution of 2008. The ceasefire agreements with

Myanmar Tatmadaw were signed in 2018, finishing many armed conflicts, which have lasted since Myanmar and India drew the demarcation line splitting Naga tribes in 1953. Not many civilians openly aspire for independence in the near future.

The question of the existence of the zone is often classified by them as having been created for the sake of Myanmar's government. It is often stressed that the Nagas populate villages and towns of the Sagain division and the Kachin state which goes beyond the area drawn by government.

(2) Photo above: A Naga woman washing the clothes in the polluted river

5. Sad past and new hopes

It was as recently as in 2009 when the Myanmar army severely beat six people for the whole day in the Lahe township for converting from Animism into Christianity, and as a result two of them died. The proclamation of freedom of speech remains in doubt. The minority policies of Myanmar are hard to predict despite Aung San Suu Kyi promising to protect the vulnerable groups.

The cruel treatment by the military that appointed itself as the safeguard of Burmese Buddhism became clear from the decades of exploitation of Naga people as the free labor for army projects. In addition, their side has reported many cases of rape and torture.

Everyone remains uncertain about the future. The desire for full-fledged democracy unleashed the civic actions among the Nagas. The inhabitants of Aung Mye Village (Khamti township) do their best to resolve the issue of the polluted river. The gold mining business turned the clean water once abundant in fish into a perilous sewage stream, causing a variety of cancer types. It remains to be seen whether the bureaucracy will stand on their side.

Moreover, some Nagas praise the transparency and lack of corruption in the road construction tendering.

6. End of isolation

The settlements of Eastern Naga tribes were isolated until WWII broke out, unlike on the Indian side, where they faced the British threat throughout XIX century. The British and Japanese armies also showed up in the areas of Htamante and Shingbwiyang, respectively.

Moving outside of the village area remains a logistical challenge; however the roads between the major townships that were once accessible only by ox cart or afoot are now developed.

The construction of the LEDO Road by the US army to Nanyun and Myanmar's own government road projects to the main towns (Leishi, Lahe, Khamti, Somra) ended the isolation of tribes after WWII. However, the general condition of Myanmar's economy during the second half of XX century did not transform their lives until recently, when the country began to flourish and the changes crawled into their communities.

(3) Photo above: The traditional Naga house

7. Backward infrastructure

Many Nagas grade the levels of hospitals and schools introduced by the central government as insufficient for the prosperity. As recently as 2017, measles killed dozens of village children in the area of Lahe township due to the lack of vaccination. Noteworthy, the local hospital labeled the outbreak at first as 'unknown'.

As in the rest of Myanmar, the unproductive slash and burn farming method (called jhuming or dengyo) requires many working hours in the fields, which keeps people from meeting their basic needs and deters further development. They are aware of the fact that these farming techniques are old-fashioned and name them as 'primitive'. A desired change is to switch from the slash-and-burn agriculture to a more sustainable model.

The Nagas are predominantly hillside farmers (subsistence farming), few of them are skilled in the household-based handicraft production such as traditional weaving of clothes and baskets.

(4) Photo below: Naga woman with the jiya (the traditional weaving device used for the production of shawls).

The agricultural products produced by the Nagas are mostly sold locally. They raise chickens and pigs, while hunting for wild animals provides an additional source of meat. Traditionally, the successful hunter shares the meat with other villagers and keeps the animal's head for oneself.

On a daily basis, the Nagas wear modern dresses often shipped along the Chindwin River from the town of Monywa, which is in Central Myanmar. Nowadays, the traditional clothing is seen as folklore to be shown off during festivals or family events.

Self-sustainability of the community is in danger. Naga farmers observe the worsening soil quality and climate change. There are accounts of landslides destroying the crop fields more frequently than in the past. In 2000, the famine near Nanyun town lasted for one year, resulting from the destruction of crops due to excessive rain. The army did not offer any help in the afflicted region.

Access to electricity and drinking water is provided in the main towns thanks to hydropower (Leishe, Nanyun) and diesel-powered projects (Khamti). The villages lack this infrastructure and are forced to resort to solar panels and river water. The households in towns and villages cook over open fire, which is detrimental to the health. To fuel it, families gather wood for many hours every week.

(5) Photo above: The traditional U-shaped winnower
(by Jejara tribe it is called Paira)

8. Settlement

The Naga traditions bear many resemblances to other tribes populating the hills of other parts of Southeast Asia. Some Nagas call the Chins and/or Kachins their younger brothers. Importantly, all of them reject the official classification as being a sub-group of the Chin people.

(6) Photo above: The Naga Hills are the homeland of the Naga people. There is no record about their origin and the migration to their present inhabitation

Nagas used to migrate in order to set up a self-sufficient village on the hills at a high elevation. The reasons for migration often came from the overpopulation of the original settlement and lack of arable lands. Most of the Nagas of Myanmar consider the territory of Western Nagas (the today Nagaland, India) to be their place of origin. The legend of the Jejara tribe says that they sustained a 3-year-drought due to a migration route that helped them find a water source.

The Makuri tribe derives its identity from a more general concept of living at the surrounding area of Mt. Saramati. The Dan Gion members believe in the tale of a forced migration caused by a conflict with the mentioned Makuris.

With the migration of the Yobami subtribe of Long Phuri Nagas, there is an oral story about the man named Yobamo that in the search of his lost mithon arrived to a new place with salty water coming out from the rock.

The Hai Mi people of Aung Mye Village close to Khamti claim to have migrated down from Nanyun as they were in need of the salt. Finding a water source was also crucial to Khamniungam tribe members. Their tribal name means 'the place where the water starts'.

Today, the Nagas from the villages often move to the townships for education, healthcare and other opportunities. Some communities work on solving the issue of accommodation for villagers but they face capital shortage (Naga Baptist Church in Khamti town).

The dominance of Burmese and Western culture is recognized, but not treated as, the danger to their own identity. However, the migration of young people to remote cities like Yangon or Mandalay, or marriage to a non-Naga person can potentially change this state of affair within one generation, as was the case of other tribes of Asia that became assimilated.

The obstacle to preserving their own culture comes also from inside. The customs differ from village to village, which makes the oral-only traditions tricky to root down in the new generations overwhelmed by Burmese media and education system.

At this moment, Burmese language serves as the lingua franca between various Naga tribes or even between family members. Since the arrival of Christianity, they are free to marry a person from other tribe that speaks a different language. The Nagamese language created to support the communication among the Western tribes is not popularized in the towns of Nagas of Myanmar.

(7) Photo above: Lahe township is populated by 30% Buddhists and 70% Baptist Christians

9. The weeded-out practices

The old ritual of headhunting is remembered by some Nagas as the fight over resources, whereas the others interpret this as a fun game or sport with no real justification. The alliances between the tribes were made to promote collaboration, if broken the blood of men; women; and children was shed. The entire villages were leveled as a result. The general unity between Nagas came well with the advent of Buddhism and Christianity. Some claim that it let them quickly abandon the old rituals. However, this declaration can be interpreted as the desired version of history. The animistic practices are reported to prevail outside of the core of religious practices such as calling for rain or sun. Hai Mi tribe members name the appeal of General Aung San as the final unity event.

Notwithstanding the New Year Festival Tof mid-January, which is to bring all Naga tribes together, some conflicts between the tribes seem to still resonate. A Long Phuri Naga tribe member describes the continuous strife of his tribe with Makuri tribe. The origin of the antagonism dates back to the headhunting times when the Makuris were forced to run away from their villages and find refuge at the village of Long Phuris. Now, because they are more numerous, Makuris are said to pose a threat to Long Phuris by banning their language and traditional dance.

(8) Photo above: Animist notions are connected to fire. It continues to be a part of the Naga New Year Festival.

10. Proselytization

The other minority groups of Myanmar, as well as the Nagas of India, began to be proselytized in the XIX century. Thanks to the missionaries, the illiteracy among those tribes could find its end and the Romanized alphabets were developed for their tribal languages which gave rise to their own literature. The isolation of Eastern Nagas resulted in the fact that the tribal languages not spoken west off Mt. Saramati lack own script. The traditions are passed down orally.

The military used to encourage Nagas to convert from Christianity to Buddhism. This could relieve them from the forced work and qualify for food support.

Nowadays, with no open missionary actions, there can be observed the competition over adherents manifesting itself in the new waves of conversion. People convert from Christianity to Buddhism (and vice versa) as well as within Christianity, for example 100 villagers from Kung Kai Lung close to Leishe township changed their faith from Baptism to Catholicism following the idea of the tribe leader.

The communities reportedly show no signs of conflict unlike in the other parts of Myanmar and Nagaland, India. In the town of Khamti populated by both Naga and Shan tribes, the regular inter-religious dialogue takes places few times a year. The leaders from other towns do not acknowledge a need for similar meetings, but all of them stress that they keep friendly relationships with the people of other religion.

The reflection of Eastern Naga's isolation is their late conversion to Christianity and Buddhism. Their old beliefs centered on the worship of spirits to whom homage could be paid practically anywhere (roadside, forest, river, etc.). Some categorize their abandoned practices as the search for the only one God.

It was as late as from 1950 to 1980's when Eastern Naga tribes began to reject the Animistic beliefs. This occurred thanks to contacts with Western Naga tribes (Baptism), Kachin missionaries (Catholicism), American missionaries (Church of Christ) and Burmese missionaries (Theravada Buddhism). This trend enforced discarding certain traditions that were difficult to reconcile with the new faith. Each case of proselytization by a missionary needed to be approved by the village chief. The conversion could be suggested by him but no tribe member refers to this as forced.

All Nagas, now proud followers of new religions do not see this development as the loss of some part of their indigenous culture. Importantly, Christianity and Buddhism did not erase all of the rituals of the forefathers.

The rituals were set to direct the life of Naga communities. The animistic practices performed by the villagers or the priest himself embraced the family life (the child birth, coming of age, engagement, marriage, divorce), healing a disease, securing the good luck, funeral, farming new land and tribal wars.

The animistic priest or Nat master could be called to appease the spirit of the potential land. Villagers could be required to sacrifice some animals and in some cases sleep in the forest for the sake of seeing a bad or good omen.

(9) Photo above: The villagers lack the access to clean water

11. Marriage

Today's marriage is governed by the universal rules of new religion. In the old times, the groom and bribe needed to belong to the same tribe which is an example of the rejected principle. The Nagas remain patriarchal in their system of marriage. The husband holds the voice on all important issues. Titles and subtitles denoting the level of kinship serve until today as prevention from incest. Some of the old customs have been woven into religious celebrations.

Jejara tribe members used to follow the three stage practice called Lai-Sui-Sui which included the engagement of babies by the exchange of their carry clothes. The second stage happened when the boy and girl were ten years old – boy's family needed to offer a dowry of six male and one female pig to girl. The marriage took place when the couple was around 14-15 years old. The ceremony included the feast during which a big rooster's neck was (and cultivates to be) cut at the time of wedding. The movement of the rooster's legs could be interpreted as the omen for the future of the newly married. The stronger movement of left leg stood for the sign of woman's dominance in the marriage, whereas the right leg symbolized the man's power. The marriage could not be cancelled based on this prejudice.

Some other tribes stress the freedom of choice by woman to select husband, but the final approval depended on the parents (the case of Makuri tribe), and their wedding celebration included a feast for the village. It was required to gift the half of all raw food to the wife's parents. In other tribes, sending a mediator to girl's family was necessary before man could propose to her (Dan Gion tribe). Wedding ceremony included the feast during which a rooster's neck was not cut, but squeezed, which served the same interpretation as in the case of Jejara tribe. In addition, an axe, a spear and a buffalo were gifted to wife's parents. All of these old practices are reported to prevail in the case of Dan Gion tribe.

On the other hand, Long Phuri tribe practiced giving shawls to girl's family, which was the prerequisite for the marriage that required paying the price in the form of a pig. The animal itself shall be split as follows: five ribs and right leg to be presented to girl's parents, and the rest to the common feast.

Hai Mi tribe members used to get engaged at the age of 10 years old by oral commitments of parents and having a meal consisting of one boiled chicken eaten by daughter's family. Marriage happened after the exchange of traditional blankets by both partners.

Thangkhul tribe member from Layshi area still practice the custom of paying the bridal price in the form of an axe, a spear, a shawl and a buffalo.

Chan subtribe (Konyak tribe) from Yinchong village used to perform the engagement practice during the New Year Festival called Aoleong which is held in some places until today, and during which the parents of daughter would call her marriage-ready and let her stay in the separate house with a piece of cloth serving as the indication of her maiden status. The spear and axe shall be passed from boy's family to the girl's as the invitation for marriage, and if accepted, the ceremony would happen soon after. The feast would also include the preparation of a chicken.

In Lainong tribe, the man's side needed to send two mediators to the woman's side to agree on the marriage. After the ceremony, one mediator would carry the things of woman. The gifts to girl's family included a shawl, a parcel of field and a cow.

12. Tribe leader back and now

Nagas have guaranteed freedom to solve the tribal issues among themselves. This resulted in the reform of the role of the tribe chief which is not hereditary anymore, but appointed by nomination by the tribe members or by volunteering. The transformation of tribal leadership in 1975 was due to the requirement set by the central government prescribing that the tribal representative shall be literate and educated. Tribe leaders often help to amicably resolve some disputes, mostly related to the land among the members of the same tribe.

(10) Photo above: Kahan (the traditional helmet consisting from tiger claws, wild boar claws, bear hairs and hornbile feathers).

In bygone times, the tribe leader would often serve in the divorce cases. He would usually name the person at fault and oversee the fulfillment of the bride's family's demands (Dan Gion tribe). Nevertheless, in the case of the Jejara tribe, only the man's and woman's families were directly involved, with the tribe chief witnessing the words of the parties.

In other cases, parents of both the man and the woman needed to come three times to the party willing to get divorced and seek an amicable solution (Long Phuri tribe). After this they had to visit the chief of the tribe, and if he failed to reconcile them, the divorce would happen after man cooks one rooster and splits it open into two parts and then sends just half of it to his wife and returns all her personal possessions.

The divorce could entail a penalty for the party at fault, such as five buffalo received at the time of wedding would become ten buffalo to be repaid by woman, if divorced. The children would stay with the man and the wife would return to her parents' house.

Chan tribe members name the principle of paying one buffalo to the girl, if the man wants the divorce. No penalty would be set for the woman desiring the divorce. In all cases, the woman would return to her parents' house.

(11) Photo above: The horns of the mithun (gayal)

13. Death

Death was an occurrence that in bygone times called for different animistic practices. Sometimes it was required that they kill the native species of the ox (mithun or gayal) to offer it to the dead spirit (Makuri tribe).

Long Phuri tribe members kept the body in the first room of the house, on the top of one large teak, with small holes underneath in order to set the fire and let it all melt down. The fire would continue for seven days and the joints would be subsequently cut, while the bones would be put into earthen bowls. Long bamboo cups served to collect the melted body liquids. After one year, the village would organize the feast for the sake of the dead person that would last two or three days and would include a meal consisting from pig or mithun on the final day. The call to the spirit of the dead was performed in order to finally expel the spirit from this world. The participants had to perform the traditional dances and set up the memorial stone with inscribed names of the dead person, parents' name and one's age.

Until now, Hai Mi tribe of Aung Mye village practice the tradition of gun shooting [called tu-me] directed to the sun and the dead was to be buried under the house.

Chan tribe members used to kill a chicken to guide the way for the spirit of the dead, following this the body was kept outside of the village on a wooden platform. After some days, only the head was brought back and boiled, the brain was to be drilled out und buried. The scalp itself was to be held in the earthen pot in the separate house.

Other tribes like Khiamniungan required the medium to communicate with the spirit and to place the dead on a teak platform which was supported by two posts in the graveyard.

14. Tattooing

The practice of tattooing often associated with the Chin people was also common among the Nagas. The tattoos on forehead, chin, below knees, on thighs were obligatory for both sexes before coming of age. There were also other rituals associated with reaching puberty, all of them are dropped but tattoos can still be found on the bodies of the members of older generations.

Long Phuri Nagas had a special ceremony. On the first day, the village chief would collect the names of boys and girls aged from 16 to 20. On the second, he would gather them separately in the morung (the traditional house with a wooden bell inside) and let them stay there with the guard.

Hai Mi tribe of Aung Mye village describes the traditional village feast with wine and rice, before which 15-year-old boys had to do a full day of hillside farming in order to be regarded as adults. In addition, one big tree from the forest was to be cut in pieces. Girls above 10 years old were to wear underwear called Lan Gaun and to be chin-tattooed and ear-pierced. That was to happen before menstruation. They also needed to help the family in farming for the whole day. The adult women needed to wear an amber stone in her ears up to old age.

Chan tribe rituals for turning into a man were the celebration ceremonies at the day of headhunting. Young men were to bring any object (even a leaf) from the enemy's territory.

Interestingly, some Nagas still make an oath by biting the handle of their knives, believing that a curse will bring the punishment in the case of violation. To the erased traditions belongs the duty of burying an egg in the soil when deciding for the construction of the house. If the egg was found with no scratches one day later, it was seen as the good omen.

(12) Photo above: Numerous villages and towns are found along the Chindwin River

15. Conclusion

Reviewing the traditions and ways of living of any indigenous tribes may allow us to define what exactly constitutes the core identity of a group.

Some Nagas describe the culture change, by comparing it to the fire, to which a new piece of wood is put in order to keep it burning.

Adaptation of outside customs raises the question of the cultural disappearance, but the separate identity of Nagas is not built upon the traditional methods of agriculture or animistic beliefs. Their identity is derived from the understanding that they all have the same ancestry. The fight against the Burmese army can serve as the pivot of their modern identity, but should be borne in mind that it does not prevent them from following the Irish example, in which they lost a chunk of their culture to the British invaders.

It is to be stressed that all indigenous people seek to deal with the contemporary world within the context of their culture. The words 'to modernize' and 'primitive' are open to many interpretations

Moreover, learning about the Nagas helps us to look back at ethnic groups of Europe, which also incorporated some old rituals into new faith, while preserving a feeling of distinction (religious syncretism).

The risk of assimilating into Burmese culture is real when we compare the quite fresh development among many tribes of Thailand such as Akha and Karen, which lose their identity due to government intervention (the schooling system), increased migration, economic developments, and as a result of innate choice. The indigenous tribes of Malaysia and Indonesia were also forced to change their lifestyle, often due to forced migration.

The Nagas want to embrace the modernity out of their own choice. The process of modernization may rescue the Naga tribes from lagging behind the other ethnic groups of Myanmar and let them reconfigure themselves in XXI century. However, that can only happen if the threats are not overlooked.

(13) Photo above: The food is prepared over the fire set on the ground inside the house.

(14) Photo above: Traditional clothing displayed during the Naga New Year Festival

References

1. The River of Lost Footsteps : A Personal History of Burma, by Thant Myint-U
2. Going Head to Head, by Boyd Matson, the January/February 2012 issue of National Geographic Traveler
3. The 2014 Myanmar Population and Housing Census, Sagaing Region
4. Cultural Change & Continuity, By Akiner
5. Modern Anthropology of South-East Asia, By Victor T. King, William D. Wilder
6. Graceffo A (2004) In an Akha Village – Living among Thailand's Largest Hill Tribe.
7. Heh NK, Tehan TM (2000) The Current Status of Akha.

How To Apply Makeup To Look Your Best In A Facebook Photo

Rachel Swan

How To Apply Makeup To Look Your Best In A Facebook Photo

This book is licensed for your personal use only. If in electronic format a separate copy of this book should be purchased for each person for whom this book is shared. Neither the author nor publisher assumes a duty of care in connection this book. Some or all of the material in this book may be fictional and for legal purposes you should treat this book as entertainment only and not for instruction.

See other books by the Author at his Amazon author page:
www.amazon.com/author/bestselling

Published by Blue Peg Publishing

If you have purchased the ebook version of this book, then please consider buying the print version if your family enjoys the ebook.

Contents

Chapter 1

More Makeup Is Better In Facebook Photos

Your Facebook profile photo is your face to the world.

All the other photos of you posted on Facebook reinforce your look and your image.

These are the images of you that your friends see first thing in the morning and the last thing at night.

They are how newcomers in your life who haven't yet met you personally gauge what kind of person you are.

These images help others them decide if you are fun-loving, beautiful, and worth getting to know better.

These are the pictures of you that more people will see than any other.

More than 500 million people around the world access Facebook regularly, and that number is continuing to climb.

That means one out of every 13 people on earth uses Facebook and more than 250 million of them log on every day.

If you are an average user, you likely already have about 130 friends on Facebook who check all your updates and send you their experiences every day. By the end of this year, you will grow that number substantially.

If you are in your teens or 20s, you likely start each day checking your Facebook and there's almost a 30 percent chance you do that before you even get out of bed. You get your news through Facebook; you chat with your friends on Facebook and you keep up with the world that really matters to you on Facebook.

All these figures add up to one thing: You should look your best in your Facebook photo.

And the key to looking your best is applying your makeup so that it emphasizes your best features.

We can teach you how to do that.

Through our easy-to-use guide, we can help you accent your best features, bring out your fullest lips and most sculptured cheekbones, and project glowing and healthy looking skin.

With a few skillful techniques gathered from expert makeup artists, we can help you create the image you want. You can look fresh-faced and natural, or darkly mysterious.

You can create a variety of looks to suit your mood, your style, and even your season.

With skillful makeup applications, you can bring out the best of your personality in your Facebook photo. Besides impressing your friends, you can impress potential employers.

Students show that more attractive people have a better chance of getting a job and are more likely to be promoted.

So whether we inherit natural, wholesome good looks or a more average face, we can bring out our best beauty with great makeup application.

Remember, your looks are what you were born with. Good or bad, they are the result of your genetic pool and nobody can change that.

But you can change your appearance. Not once, not twice, but many, many times.

Chances are you already are quite skilful at applying your makeup to glam up your appearance in real life. But did you know different rules apply when you get ready for a photo shoot?

For example, for day to day wear you may use a light hand to apply your makeup. But to achieve the same look in your Facebook photo, more makeup is essential.

Think about the amount of makeup you use normally, and then consider how much more makeup you use for a special event like a prom or for being part of a wedding party.

Now ramp that up another notch to get the best results in your Facebook photo.

If you do not apply enough makeup and in the proper way, you will look washed out in your Facebook photo.

In the coming chapters, we will take you step-by-step from foundation to blush to eyeliner to lips to bring out your best you.

But first, it's important to start a basic beauty routine now so that whatever Facebook image you decide to project, you will have the basics to build from.

Start now by making good skin care part of your life-long habit.

Here are 10 things you can begin to do right away to build your best possible skin, the canvas on which all your exciting new beauty looks will be created:

1. Drink at least two litres of water every day. Water hydrates your body and keeps your skin soft and glowing.
2. Stick to a healthy diet rich in fresh fruit and vegetables.
3. Ensure that you get sufficient sleep every night, between seven and nine hours for normal healthy teens.
4. Have regular facials at least once every six months if your budget allows it.
5. Use cleansers that are specially designed to protect your skin from the normal breakouts that accompany the teen years.
6. Know and understand your skin type and the routines that will keep it clear and healthy. See your doctor for recommendations if acne is a persistent problem.
7. Maintain a daily exercise routine and whenever possible, spending at least 30 minutes a day walking in the fresh air.
8. Limit the amount of caffeine and alcohol that your drink. These products can dry and age your skin.
9. Avoid exposing your skin to either extreme heat or cold.
10. Use a mask regularly on your face and neck.

Once you have made good skin care a basic part of your beauty routine, the next step is excellent makeup application.

We will take you through the techniques to present your best face and encourage you to take time to practice and experiment with different effects.

If you have a digital camera, try techniques we will recommend and then photograph yourself and download it to your computer so you can see how what you try will work on the Facebook screen.

Try your new look in different poses until you are comfortable with it.

Get a few friends together and practice your makeup styles together. Photograph each other and print a few of your favorite looks on photo paper. Tack them up on a board and vote on which looks you and your friends should post on Facebook.

Chapter Two

Start With What Doesn't Show

Have you ever seen photos of movie stars without their makeup?

Every so often some persistent photographers find them out with their faces au naturel and capture them for the entire world to see.

It's a pretty startling contrast to the glamorous image we are used to see them project. Even Angelina Joli, Miley

Cyrus and Kate Hudson look ordinary without the benefit of the makeup artist's touch.

Their features, as beautiful as they are, are not displayed to their best without the art of makeup. With skillful touches here and there, they are transformed to dazzle us.

You can do that too.

The most basic rule of being beautiful is understanding that what is underneath really matters, whether it is our skin, our bodies, or our personalities.

That is the secret the most photographed women in the world know.

Lady Gaga, who often performs wearing gigantic glasses that hide much of her face, is so convinced that her whole look matters that she insists her make-up artist do dramatic eye makeup and full lashes behind those shades, even if she doesn't plan to take them off.

So you too need to start at the beginning, with your beautiful bare face. From that canvas, we are going to slowly and skillfully build a look that will dazzle your Facebook fans and present your most attractive face to the world.

The story begins with your face and a mirror.

Look at your naked face in the mirror. Turn left, turn right. Study your profile. Study the shape of your face, the features which are most prominent and the beautiful features that aren't standing out naturally as well as you would like.

Under your skillful touch, you will build on this naked face to create a dazzling look for your Facebook photo.

The first step is to cleanse your skin thoroughly.

Then study your skin texture. Is it dry or oily? Are you prone to acne?

It is important to understand this from the start, because the makeup techniques for the most glorious you depend on building from one of these two skin care foundations.

If your skin is dry, for example, the number one beauty technique that will supersede all others is to moisturize it by gently rubbing in moisturizing cream for three to five minutes before you start to apply concealer and then makeup.

Singer Selena Gomez, whose skin must endure constant travel but must always look healthy and glowing when she is photographed, reportedly takes two bottles of moisturizing lotion with her wherever she goes.

On the other hand, if your skin is oily and prone to break-outs, thoroughly cleanse it with a product specifically designed for preventing acne. Once the cleansing is completed, apply a layer of acne prevention cream over your face, gently rubbing it in for a couple of minutes. Then let it dry three to five minutes.

Follow this by applying a concealer.

Why use a concealer?

Its primary purpose is to hide any blemishes or skin discolorations. But for use in photos, it also hides any discoloration around your eyes and your lips.

It is important that when your makeup is complete that your concealer is hidden. That means that under normal day-to-day conditions, you would select a concealer that closely matches your skin tone or is just one shade lighter.

However, when doing your makeup for your Facebook photo, there is a significant change to this established procedure. To accommodate the camera's impact, the concealer you apply as a basis for your photo should be two to three times lighter than your normal skin tone.

There are so many concealers on the market, how do you know which one will work best for you? If your budget permits, select a few. One with a slightly yellow tone is best for hiding mild blemishes or skin discolorations like bruises or birthmarks, but one with a pink or peach tone is best for concealing under-eye darkness.

A shade that's really close to your skin tone is best for covering red pimples. Or, because green neutralizes red, some people pick a green-toned concealer to hide red acne.

Darker concealers are best for hiding puffiness in your skin or under your eyes.

But keep in mind that all of these tinted concealers work a little differently on people with different skin tones. A peach-tone concealer will hide splotches on a person with darker skin, for example. It is best to experiment with a few kinds to see what works best on you as an individual.

Concealers come in liquids, creams and sticks. Generally speaking, the liquids are best for people with dry skins but they also provide the lightest amount of coverage.

Creams are best for people with oily skin and they are the easiest to blend seamlessly into your skin. The sticks may be the most convenient to tuck into your purse, and they are the most opaque, hiding a multitude of problems.

Regardless of whether you use a liquid, cream or stick concealer, there is a good procedure for using it effectively.

The secret of creating the flawless complexion look is blending your concealer so it doesn't look obvious. In the case of getting ready for your Facebook photo, it will show a bit more than usual, but that's because you are going to use more makeup than usual.

The trick is to apply it in sheer layers and always gently spread it in with a sponge.

Place several dots of concealer under your eyes. Then, using a pad and your middle finger, tap it in gently. Never rub in concealer. Always just tap it gently.

Apply more dots of concealer to your chin area, and around your nose and mouth if you need to hide any imperfections there. There is no need to scrimp on this product.

A good concealer is really the most important product in your makeup kit. Some stars actually carry concealer tucked into their purses instead of foundation in case of emergency touch-ups.

Remember that if you are taking your Facebook photo in the summer months, and you are a person out in the sunshine quite a bit, your skin tone may naturally be a bit darker than it normally is.

If you have unnatural skin redness or rashes, dab the concealer in place to hide these skin imperfections. If you rely solely on makeup, they can actually look worse. Select a concealer that is sold as a "stay put" product in the case of rashes.

If you have acne scars or other scars to conceal, you can minimize them by using a darker concealer to hide the lighter areas of scarring. If the scar is darker in colour, use a lighter shade of concealer. Either way, the key is the careful tapping in of the product to the scar itself and the recessed area beside it.

A common problem is dark circles under the eyes. These sometimes occur sporadically because of lack of sleep or illness, but some women have a predisposition to them genetically.

Use a brightening concealer under the eyes to enhance the light in this delicate area. Be careful not to rub the skin; just tap gently.

Remember to let the concealer set for about 10 seconds before you begin to blend it.

If you are trying to cover a blemish with green concealer, remember that the idea here is that because red and green are opposite from each other on the color wheel, they will cancel each other out. That's the theory.

To make it happen in practice, dab green concealer on bright red blemishes. Never rub it. Just pat it gently with a clean makeup sponge to blend it thoroughly.

Chapter 3

Finding The Right Foundation

Your natural beauty and freshness needs to shine through on your Facebook photo, but there's no reason you can't hike it up a notch to enhance your "wow" factor. Think of your face as a creative canvass that you will build on to bring out the very best you.

Getting the right foundation is an essential part of the process. The perfect foundations work to even out your skin tone and get rid of small imperfections so that your face is completely flawless.

You may have to do a bit of experimenting with your look and try taking shots of yourself with your digital camera to see which techniques work best.

In the best case scenario, your foundation will merely be the cover to your healthy skin. Keep your skin naturally glowing by drinking at least six to eight glasses of water a day. Water hydrates your body and keeps your skin soft.

Stick to a healthy diet rich in fresh fruit and vegetables, and get between seven and nine hours of sleep each night.

If your budget permits, get regular facials at least four times a year. Exfoliate your face and neck about once a week to rejuvenate your skin.

Know and understand your skin type and the routines that will serve to keep it clear and healthy-looking. Seek a doctor's advice if you are struggling with either severe acne or dryness. A great deal can be done to help you.

Maintain a daily exercise routine and when possible, spend at least 30 minutes a day walking in the fresh air.

Limit the amount of caffeine and alcohol that you drink. These products can dry and age your skin.

Avoid exposing your skin to either extreme heat or cold.

Every day clean, tone and moisturize your skin and use a mask regularly on your face and neck.

When it comes to selecting the right foundation from the hundreds on the market for your Facebook photo, opt for a liquid matte foundation, especially if your skin is inclined to be oily.

Match the type of foundation to your skin type. If your skin is oily, make sure you select an oil-free foundation. If your skin is dry, you may be better off with a moisturizing base foundation or even a combination one.

Next comes the process of getting the color right.

The biggest mistake people make is selecting a shade too far away from their natural skin tone. Under normal circumstances, always pick the shade closest to your natural coloring.

For your Facebook photo, however, you should choose a shade just slightly darker than you usually would wear.

Before you apply your foundation, make sure that it is at room temperature. Also, make sure that your hands and face are clean, and ideally, that it has been at least 20 minutes since you applied any moisturizer. If you put foundation directly over moisturizer, it may just slide off.

Put the makeup on your face in a series of small dots to your cheeks, nose tip, forehead, and chin.

Then apply your foundation with a makeup brush, using light strokes moving upwards across your face. The foundation brush is gentle and it will keep your skin from flaking.

Blend your foundation completely to the edges of your face and years, your neck and hairline, paying special attention to the jaw and hairline, as these are the areas people most often make mistakes on.

If you are wearing a tank top or if you neck colour is lighter than your face, you should spread the foundation evenly over your neck and even your shoulders as well if they will appear in the photo.

This gives you a pulled-together look and overall, a more natural appearance.

Then thoroughly wash your cosmetic sponge and set it to dry. If you do not follow this part of the procedure, your sponge will become a breeding ground for bacteria.

Hint:

A matte foundation applied with a flat top brush is a favored choice for a great photo shoot. By wearing a little more makeup than you would normally wear, you will avoid looking washed out in your photo.

Chapter 4

Puff And Pat: Picking The Proper Powder

The importance of powder to looking your best in a Facebook photo cannot be overstressed. But for many people, it is the missing tool in their makeup kit.

If you are youthful, you may have a built-in aversion to it because of an association with Victorian times when books are sprinkled with references of women wishing to go "powder their noses," and when washrooms were actually called "powder rooms."

As well, there is such a variety of powder products on the market that to the uninitiated, it is overwhelming. Where to you even start to find the right one for you? It is a mystery that many people don't bother to solve. They just avoid it altogether.

And that is a mistake when it comes to looking your best in your Facebook photo.

It is essential to dust translucent or loose powder lightly all over your face once you have applied your foundation. This achieves five important beauty secrets for you:

- It sets your concealer and foundation so it stays put, lasting longer and never streaking.
- It removes shine and oil that distorts your features on camera.
- It smoothes out the elements between each makeup element, from your foundation to your blush to your eyes, and gives you a look of oneness.
- It acts as an overall concealer of any flaws, toning down mistakes such as too much blush on your cheeks.
- It protects your skin from the harshness of sun and cold as it conceals flaws and open pores.

But you have to really understand how to do it right or it can be your biggest makeup flaw ever.

Remember the infamous pictures of actress Nicole Kidman walking out onto the red carpet at the premiere of her latest film Nine with white powder clearly visible on her nose and cheeks.

By the next day, the tabloids and blogs were abuzz with news about her "makeup malfunction." They used words like "Coker Face" to describe the usually immaculate Australian actress.

Of course, the explanation from makeup artists around the world was that either the 42-year-old mother-of-three, or her make-up artist, did not blend her powder properly before heading onto the red carpet for her second round of photographs.

Don't let that happen to you in your Facebook photo.

Remember that nothing sets your concealer and makeup in place better than translucent powder. But it has to be properly applied. Make-up, even when it is heavy, must never look "made-up."

When you look at photos of movie stars, they look glamorous and beautiful, and their makeup has a natural, effortless look.

Good face powder is the secret to either getting or losing this flawless, perfectly natural look. Applied properly, it is completely invisible, but it holds your great look perfectly in place.

You may want to use it more than once in the makeup application process. Apply it over your concealer and foundation, and also a tiny bit over your eyelids, your lips and chin and your forehead to prevent shine.

Apply it to your neck to make sure that there is no line between your face and neck that creates an unnatural look. Even dab a bit on your ears if their color is different from your face.

This is particularly important when you are doing your makeup for a Facebook photo. You want flawless, not distortion because the camera has focussed on the shine.

Make sure that you keep your powder brush or applicator clean. Change it frequently so that it doesn't get dirty with oil or dirt from your face. Using a dirty brush could cause infection or irritation to your skin.

Sheer, fine and colorless, translucent powder comes in many different shades to match all skin tones.

When you go to purchase it, you will find you have three options: loose powder, pressed powder and mineral powder.

Keep a container of the loose powder at home when you are setting your foundation. It is really most effective and easy to use. It works well for both normal skin and oily skin.

It is great in particular if you suffer from acne, since it actually absorbs oil and smoothes your skin, adding colour, even though it is translucent.

But here are two tips to remember about loose powder.

First, apply it before you get dressed. It has a tendency to float a bit through the air and could land on that black top you are wearing. Use it before getting dressed for the day.

Second, it is most inconvenient to carry in your makeup kit or purse, since its potential to spin and cover everything is enormous. In that case, opt instead for a small compact of pressed powder that comes with a small brush to be used for touch-ups throughout your day.

Pressed powder comes in the traditional compact and is excellent for tucking into your makeup bag or purse or pocket. It is particularly effective in covering problem areas on your skin.

For example, if you have dark circles under your eyes, or your skin has red patches from a rash or acne, it is excellent at concealing this. For the purposes of your Facebook photo, you will want to use it as a sealant for your concealer and foundation, but it can also be used in other circumstances over your bare skin for quick touch-ups. This is good only if your skin is not too oily.

The newest kind of powder on the market is mineral powder, but it is not particularly recommended for use when you are being photographed.

However, in other circumstances, it provides long coverage and it won't clog your pores. Older women use it more frequently to decrease the look of fine lines on their faces.

Match the color of powder you purchase as closely as possible to the color of your foundation. Test the color in the store by applying it to the back of your hand.

Once you get used to powder's benefits, it will become a natural addition to your makeup book.

Chapter 5

Using Blush To Bring Out Your Best Features

Singer Katy Perry loves to switch up her look. One day she's blonde and sultry, the next day she's girl next door brunette and retro and before you get that image fixed in your mind, she's pink-haired and cotton-candy makeup.

Katy reportedly loves her red lips and liquid eyeliner, but one of her favorite beauty tools is her blush. Her secret is to always smile to find the apples of your cheeks before applying it.

She's not the only heavily-photographed star to swear by the beauty powers of blush and bronzer. In fact, for most people facing the cameras regularly, it is the most versatile thing in their cosmetic bag.

Don't scrimp on it if you want to look your best in your Facebook photo because it is the secret ingredient in creating a radiant face.

The flash of a camera can make your skin looked washed out, but the skillful use of bronzer and blush can prevent that.

With a few brush strokes you can bring beauty and dimension to your face in a photograph. You can outline your facial structure and set off your most striking features.

Blushers also enhance your facial beauty by giving you that look of rosy-cheeked health, provided you match them as close as possible to your skin tone.

If you have pale, almost porcelain skin, for example, you should avoid a dark red blush or you will end up looking like a store mannequin.

A good trick is to pinch your cheeks lightly and see the color they turn. That is the color you should look for in your blush. Another tip if you are worried about selecting the wrong color is just to match it to your lipstick color.

Considering that you are wearing more makeup than usual for your Facebook photo, you still need to match the color as closely as possible to your overall look. If your skin is creamy colored, wear a pink or coral blush. If it is dark, wear wine or burgundy blush.

When you go to purchase blush, the displays can be intimidating. Not only does blush come in a wide variety of colors, it is also available in both powders and creams.

Which is best for you and why?

If you have slightly oily skin, a powder is likely your best choice. It is easy to apply as well. If your skin is dryer, go for the cream.

Some people avoid blush altogether because they have seen it so badly apply, huge circles of red in the middle of faces that look contrived and artificial.

All you need to do to use blush effectively to enhance your face is to learn the technique.

That means never applying blush in the middle of your cheeks because it will give you the clown effect. You know you've overdone it when your friends start asking if you feel unwell because you look fevered.

Instead, gently follow the structural line of your cheekbones. To locate your cheekbones, suck in your cheeks. Place your finger gently to your face and feel the edge of the cheekbone. You will feel the exact spot where you should apply the blush to keep your cheekbones prominent and enhance your overall beauty.

Want to check if you have applied it correctly? Stand in front of the mirror and smile heartily enough that your cheekbones go up. What you see now in the mirror is the "apple" of your cheeks. The blush should be on the apple of the cheek and brushed lightly up towards your hear and hairline.

If you face is quite full, put the blush at the outside of your face, close to your temples. If your cheekbones are high, put the blush in the center of your face.

Add a little bit of blush down your cheeks, over your nose and chin and even your forehead for a gently, healthy glow. To accent your face for your photo, also apply blush underneath the cheekbone and some on your temple.

The effect of blush applied to the apples of your cheeks is that your skin looks clearer and your eyes look bigger.

If your face is quite long and narrow, use blush to give an added dimension of width. Apply your blush to the lower part of your cheekbone at a horizontal angle. Apply more blush color only on the outer side of your cheeks.

That is because color added to the middle of the face will make your face look even longer, not the effect you are trying to achieve.

Sometimes it is suggested to add highlighting powder on top of the blush, but avoid it before photographs because it will make your skin look shiny.

After the blush, add bronzer for a glowing, healthy look under normal circumstance. Brush it across your forehead, your chin and down your nose. However, when you are preparing to be photographed, leave that step out.

You do not want any kind of makeup that leaves a shine, for the camera will pick that up and focus on it in an unflattering way.

Resist the temptation to spread your blush with your fingertips because the brush is much better suited to this task. If will spread it thoroughly and professionally without damaging your skin in any way.

Once you have had your Facebook photo taken, if you want to tone down your blush, just use a cotton ball or makeup brush to remove the excess. A bit of natural color powder will also tone it down, as will a dab of foundation.

Chapter 6

Pucker Up: Secrets Of Sensuous Lips

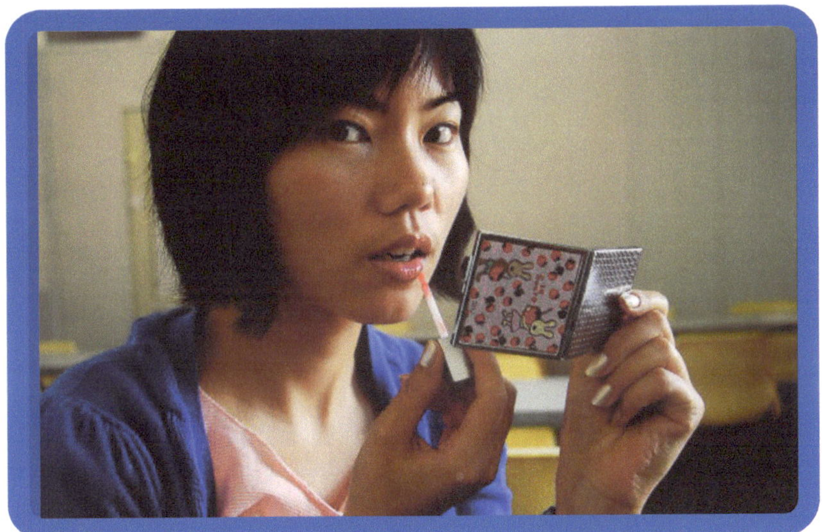

Do you remember playing "dress-up" as a child? You got into your mom's lipstick and carefully applied it, but the end result always look like a red flood that left your lips and overflowed onto their surrounding skin.

Endearing as you may have looked as a child, you do not want this makeup faux pas to appear in your Facebook photo. If you are not careful, your lipstick just jumps into the tiny lines around your mouth.

Makeup specialists call this effect "lipstick bleed." It is easily prevented if you follow these steps:

- Pat translucent powder on your lips before you use any kind of lipstick or lip gloss.
- Rub a natural-colored lip pencil all over your lips before you apply any lipstick.
- Apply lip liner matching your lipstick around your lips to create a barrier to stop the bleed.
- Apply your lipstick with a brush instead of layering it on directly from the stick or tube. Start at the centre of your lower lip and work outward with small, delicate strokes. Then do the same with the top lip.
- Use your fingers to gently tap in your lipstick.
- Put a bit of translucent powder on top of your lipstick to hold it in place.

If you check your makeup at any time and find that your lipstick is bleeding, simply grab a paper towel, moisten it lightly, and wipe off all of the lipstick. Add foundation or powder to cover the bleed stain.

When you reapply your lipstick, stay away from the corners and edges of your mouth.

It is important to practice putting on your lipstick and experimenting with different kinds to be sure that it will stay in place without creating a mess to your otherwise beautifully made up face.

In the best circumstances, the lipstick will complete your makeup. In many cases, if you use darker tones and have full and beautiful lips, it will enhance one of your most beautiful features.

You likely already have a favorite shade of lipstick because almost everybody does.

For example, singer Nicki Minaj is so fond of her staple pink lipstick that she once said she didn't know what she would ever do if they stopped making it.

But for your Facebook photo, you may have to venture out of your comfort zone.

Your lipstick color should be at least one shade deeper than you normally wear. If you usually favor a natural look, wearing only nude lip color or pale pink, you have to abandon that look temporarily. It will leave you looking very washed out in your photo.

Instead, go for a mauve or red lip liner and lipstick.

If you normally use lip gloss instead of lipstick, consider changing your products before your Facebook photo is taken. Gloss is shiny and as a general rule does not photograph as beautifully as the more opaque lipstick.

If the camera is not a consideration, lip gloss will make your lips appear a little fuller and gives them a sexy, subtle shine.

Likewise, avoid all frosted lip colors. They will hardly show up in your photo and you will look like you have no lipstick on at all.

Chapter 7

How To Make The Most Of Your Eyes

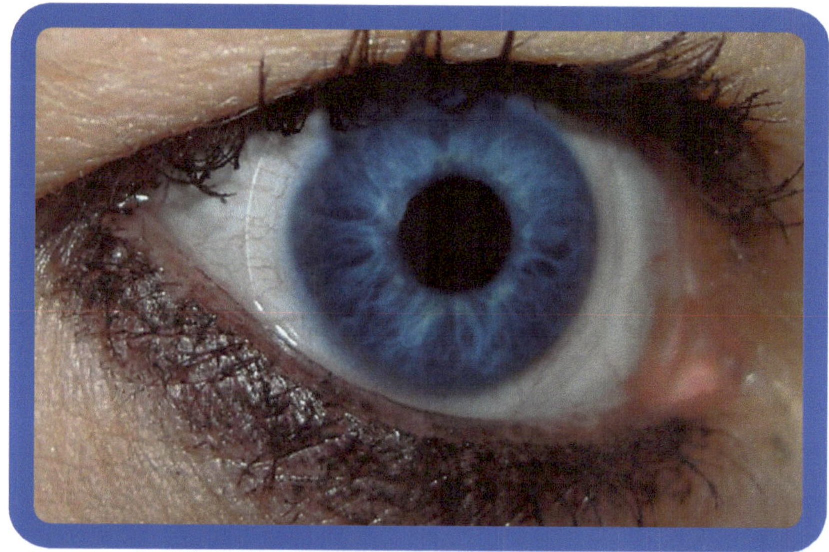

One of the most interesting and fun aspects of preparing your makeup for your Facebook photo is developing a signature eye look.

All the top performers have one, and some have several.

For example, Debby Harry, front woman of the all-male rock band Blondie, is famous for her smoky eyed look. She creates it by using a contour shadow above the lid and using light colored shadow, then layering on lots of smoky liner around the upper and lower lash lines.

British songstress Adele has become famous for her cat-eye look created by extending her upper and lower lid liquid liner to meet past the end of her eyes. It has the effect of perfectly accenting her lovely almond shaped eyes.

Build your own look from the assumption that it is almost impossible to use too much eye makeup when it comes to creating your best face for a photo. Clever use of liner, shadow and mascara can add up to an eye that captivates the viewer.

Your eyes and your lips really are the two features viewers of your Facebook photo will focus on.

To get started you will need mascara, a creamy shadow, and a liquid liner.

Mascara

Before applying your mascara, comb your eyelashes to separate them.

Then gently roll your brush over a paper towel to remove excess mascara. You do not want your eyelashes clumping together. If you don't have a paper towel, use a napkin. A piece of toilet paper or facial tissue won't do. Both have a bit of lint on them and you could end up irritating your eyes, particularly if you wear contact lenses.

Many people apply their mascara with a series of short, quick strokes. This does not give the best effect. Instead, use a slow-motion gentle sweep over the top of your lashes starting from the base of your eyelashes and working out to the tips.

Stop. Check the effect and let the mascara dry for a minute. Nine times out of 10, one application is all that you will need.

Then comb your lashes again to break them apart and remove any clumps of mascara.

If you want to add more color or drama, give your lashes a second or even third coating, but follow the same procedure, allowing them to dry in between applications and combing them to avoid clumping.

Singer and actress Miley Cyrus uses more than one mascara application to get her beautiful, full-lash look that is so dramatic it could be mistaken for false lashes. She reportedly uses a metal lash comb to separate them and avoid clumping between applications of mascara.

If you have a problem with your mascara clumping, it could be your application technique or it could be the mascara itself. If you have been using the mascara for a long time, it may be getting dried and flaky. As a general rule, it should be replaced every three months.

If you have been using it for more than two months and you are starting to have problems, throw it out and get a replacement.

You may mistakenly promote the clumping of mascara by pumping the brush in and out of the tube several times when you are getting ready to apply it. There is no need for this and it is, in fact, not a good idea at all. When you move the brush in and out of the tube several times, you are not "stirring" up the mascara and making it more fluid. Instead, you are forcing more air into the tube and drying the mascara. It will last even less than three months before it starts to clump if you do this regularly.

If your mascara tends to run or transfers itself to the skin under your eye, try not applying any mascara to your lower lashes. If you get caught in the rain or high humidity, or shed a tear in an emotional situation, this is where it will start to run.

If you want to use mascara on your lower lid for effect in your Facebook photo, and that is advisable for maximum drama, just be careful to check that it is not running once the camera starts clicking.

Remember that even when you select waterproof mascara, it can still run under certain circumstances. If you have a quick cry or something gets in your eye and tears com and create little rivulets down your cheeks, blot it away before it dries and sticks. (Beauty experts suggest you do not use waterproof mascara exclusively because some formulas can dry out your lashes.)

If it has already settled onto your skin, use a bit of moisturizer or water to mix with your foundation, rub out the mascara and gently blend the makeup over it.

Eye shadow

For a dramatic look for your Facebook photo, select a powder or cream eye shadow that is in contrast to the color of your eyes.

For example, if you eyes are blue, you might want to try taupe on the eyelid to widen your eyes and a chocolate brown just above that. A bronze color would work well for you too, but be sure to avoid for a photo the shimmery, shiny bronzes that will distort your look through the camera's lens.

Brown-eyed girls should use either a deep forest green or a navy or dark sapphire for eye shadow appeal.

If your eyes are green, experiment with a lavender color on the lids. Other options for the darker shades are eggplant or burgundy. For hazel eyes, try pale and darker green shades.

Stick to these colors regardless of what you are wearing. It is not essential any longer that your eye makeup should match the color of your clothing.

You may be tempted to want to overdo the dark and smoky look for your photo but you should experiment with it first and see if it really works for you. In some cases it is the perfect choice, adding drama and excitement to your big, beautiful eyes.

However, if your eyes are smaller and you overdo the smoky look, you will not be happy with the result. Your eyes will look even tinier than they really are. Heavy dark eyeliner, even if it is smudged in and softened, can close up your eyes if it is applied top and bottom.

When applying eye shadow, start with coverage of the eyelid and then add another line above your eye but just below your eyebrow.

Use light shades in these two spots because it will make your eyes look larger and will draw people into your face. You can use darker shadow at the crease of the eyes and just above that if you wish.

The lighter color right next to your eyes makes them appear larger. A darker color on your lid, when photographed, darkens your eyes and can sometimes make you look tired.

Eyeliner

You have three choices when it comes to eyeliner: pencils, liquids and powder-based liners. There are also powdered cream eyeliners.

All of them can help you create dramatic looks for your eyes and you may have a personal preference because you are comfortable using certain products.

But if you want to go for drama and are flexible, liquid eyeliners are one of the easiest ways to get the look you want. They are easy to handle and you can immediately see the effect, they stay in place for long periods of time without bleeding out into tiny lines that might be around the eyes, and they can really accent your eyes and make them your most memorable feature.

Liquid liners flow easily onto your eyelid without having to pull it. Because many of them are waterproof as well, they stay put under studio lights when your photograph is being taken.

For best results with eye liner, apply it with a firm, steady hand starting from the outside of the lower part of the eyelid, extending about three quarters of the length toward the inner part. Unless your eyes are very large, do not extend all the way to the other end of your eye, since it will give the appearance of being closed and smaller.

You may want to add liner to the lower eye as well, but if your eyes are small, this could make them look smaller.

You may find it more effective just to dot a tiny bit of liquid liner in several places under your eye and gently dab it so you do not have a full, hard line effect.

If you want to make your eyes appear larger, you can extend the top line out and up a tiny bit at the sides, blending it into your shadow.

To bring out smaller eyes, line the crease above the eye with either liquid or pencil liner as well.

If you do not like the effect of the dark liner,

When you use mascara, shadow and liner, remember to remove all of them before you go to sleep. Use eye makeup removers or specially formulated makeup remover clothes and pat gently, never rubbing, to ensure that your makeup is gone before you sleep.

Chapter 8

What To Pack In Your Touch-Up Kit

When your makeup is done and you are ready to have your photo taken, don't leave home without your touch-up kit.

What should you pack to ensure that you have the proper tools on hand to do a quick-fix if you need to while your Facebook photo is being taken?

Unless you plan to lug around a suitcase, you have to make choices between what you must have and what you would like to have. This chapter will help you do that so that your makeup kit is efficient and not too cumbersome to carry.

You need a mirror so you can do quick checks on your makeup. You also need powder, over and above all else, and often it comes in a compact with a mirror, so you can easily combine these two essential items.

Next to powder, which should be used repeatedly to ensure that your skin does not become too shiny, your concealer is a "must have." Even if your photos are being taken by a friend, you may find when you look at the first attempts that some imperfection needs a quick cover before you smile into the lens again.

Normally your foundation makeup will last for several hours, but it is a good insurance policy to tuck it into your emergency pack as well.

Bring your lip liner and lip color, your eye shadow and your liquid eye liner. Your mascara should last all day, so it is not necessary to bring it along.

Tuck in your blush and bronzer in case despite your model makeup attempts you look too pale in your photos.

You may not think of tweezers, but they can be quite an asset when you suddenly discover the one eyebrow hair that has a mind of its own.

A bit of moisturizer cream is handy to have in case you discover a last minute bit of patchy skin, and it never hurts to have a makeup wipe in case you suddenly have to do a quick makeover for a different look.

After all, you really can't imagine the results until you have tried and seen the results.

Beauty experts often tuck in a spare nail polish as well, in case you get a chip and want to be photographed resting on your hands under your chin.

When you are doing your Facebook photo, the last thing you want is a limitation on your poses. If the photographer has an idea, you want to be able to try it without worrying that your nails won't look their best.

Be sure to carry liquid products like nail polish and foundation in separate plastic bags or containers within your makeup kit.

You don't need a vivid imagination to consider how your makeup will be affected, for example, if orange polish spills all over it.

If you have long hair, you might want to tuck in a couple of hair clips or pony tail holders in case you want to vary your look just to see the effect. Tuck in a comb and brush for last minute hair touch-ups as well.

Even though you take the time to do your model makeup at home, you can ensure that your photo shoot goes smoother and more efficiently if you tuck these items into your makeup bag before you head out to get your Facebook photo taken.

This is also a good exercise for preparing a well-organized and effective makeup bag that you can transfer from purse to purse on other days.

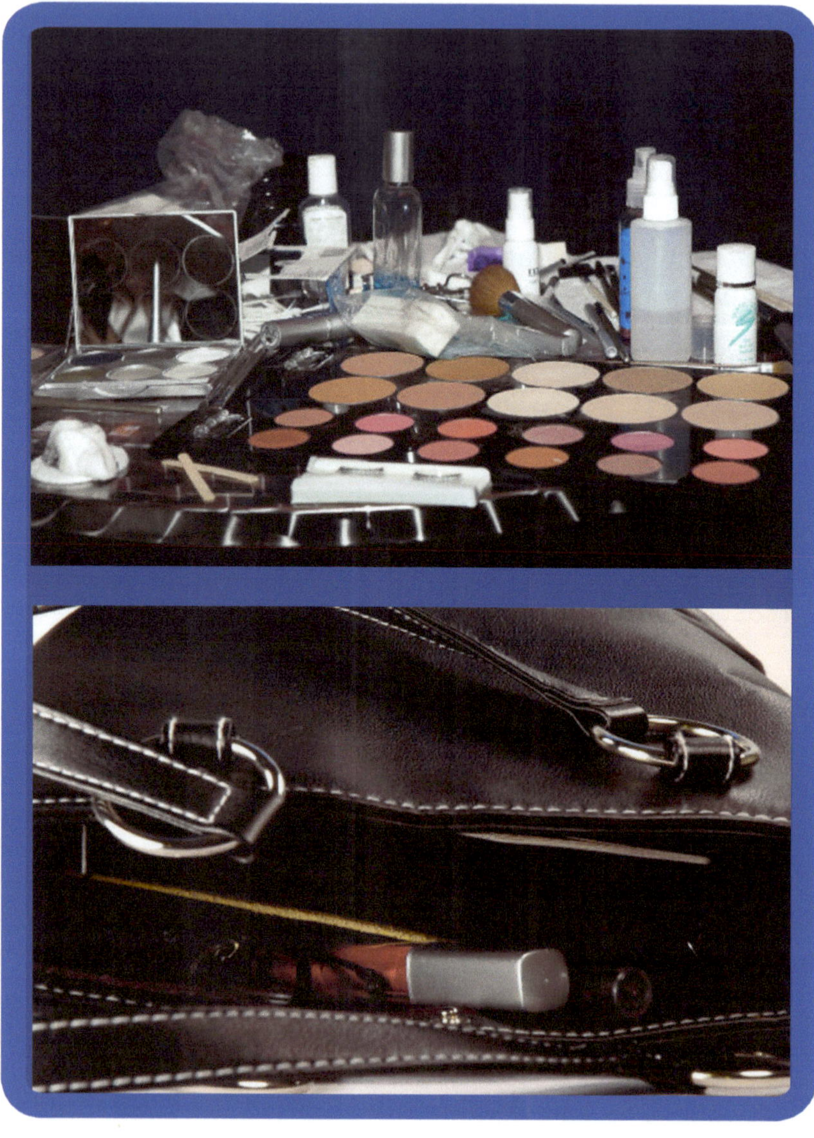

Chapter 9

Dos And Don'ts Of Applying Makeup For Your Facebook Photo

Think you've got a good plan for your Facebook photo look now? Here's our master checklist to ensure that you have all the do's in hand and avoided all the don'ts.

DO

Do wear more makeup than you normally would when you are getting your Facebook photo taken.

Do remember that you want people to recognize you. Your makeup is supposed to enhance your real beauty, not turn you into somebody even your mother won't recognize.

Do decide which feature on your face you want to accent and focus on it. Usually it is your lips or your eyes. Pick one and build everything else to work with that look.

Do make sure that your makeup is blended into your neck, your ears, and your hairline. You want to have a complete look, not a dark face over a snow-white neck.

Do use eyeliner even if you don't normally bother. You need to enhance your eyes to bring them out in the photo.

Dab concealer on your eyelids and lips before applying eye shadow and lipstick to reduce the possibility of the color "bleeding" out to the fine lines around your lips and eyes.

Do keep dabbing your face with translucent powder between shots to ensure that your face is not shiny.

Do pick eye shadow colors that do not match your eyes, but instead enhance them.

Do bring concealer with you at all times for quick corrections of blemishes or imperfections.

Do get sufficient sleep before posing for your Facebook photo. All the makeup in the world can't really cover tired. It has a way of oozing out.

DON'T

Don't wear black lip liner. Trendy though it may be, it will not show up in your photo.

Don't wear frosted lip colors. They may be natural and charming in the light of day, but they will hardly show up at all in your photo.

Don't wear frosted eye shadows. They will not look good in your photo.

Don't try any new skin product less than 48 hours before getting your photo taken. You don't want an unexpected allergic reaction to cause an unexpected rash or redness in your face for your photos.

Don't wear pale pink lipstick. It may look lovely under other circumstances, but it will give you a washed out look in your photos.

Don't forget to get relaxed before to the photo session starts. Smile all the way inside of yourself, so that your eyes are happy and glowing as well as your lips.

Don't over-accessorize. Your Facebook photo is really going to be all about your face, so don't have anything competing with it for people's attention.

Don't skip the eye liner just because you don't normally wear it. Make an exception this time and experiment with different looks to draw people to your eyes.

Don't use your fingertips to put on blush and eye shadow. Use a brush to smooth them on so you do not rough up these delicate skin areas.

Don't be tense when your photo is taken. It's just a picture, after all. If you don't like it, try again. Tenseness has a way of hardening your face despite your best makeup efforts.

Chapter 10

Common Flaws And How To Fix Them

You think you did everything right, but just as you are ready to pose for your Facebook photo, you see a flaw. Here's a last minute guide to how to fix six common makeup flaws and ensure that you look your best for your online friends.

Your head doesn't look like it belongs on your neck

You've gone to great lengths to create a dramatic, glamorous face. Your eyes sparkle and look out in a way you can hardly imagine is you. Your cheekbones are showing off their fine structure and your perfectly lined lips are full and sensuous.

Just when you think this is as good as it gets, you look at yourself from another angle in the mirror and suddenly realize your head doesn't go with the rest of your body, especially your neck.

Your darker than usual foundation, your darker than usual blush, and your more prominent than usual makeup didn't take into account that your neck is white as alabaster.

Quick Fix:

Apply a few drops of foundation on your neck. Blend with a brush, gently sweeping up to your jaw line until there is no demarcation line between the two. Insure the fix holds by patting on translucent powder.

You look sick

You did your best to find the perfect foundation and create your look from there. But instead of glowing good looks, you have a slightly sick appearance.

You may have purchased a makeup shade that just does not work on your skin.

There are a number of reasons this can happen, with the most common one being that the lights in the store where you purchased it had a yellow or reddish glow to them, giving you a different perception of the makeup you were buying.

This can also happen because you normally test makeup on your hand, and in summer especially, the skin tone on your hand may be considerably darker than the skin on your face.

Sometimes certain types of medical treatments or medications seem to affect your skin tone as well.

Quick fix:

Try first to add a bit more blush and bronzer and see if you can alter the shade sufficiently to complete your photo. If you still do not look well, you have no choice but to go back to the store and try another shade or two until you get a foundation that sets off your skin to its best advantage.

When purchasing cosmetics, dab a bit of the tester on your hand and then walk to the closest window where you can see it in natural light. It might also help to check the color against your jaw law instead of your hand if your hand is a lot darker than your face.

That's why it's a good idea to have a practice session before getting your Facebook photo taken.

You look overly-surprised

Have you ever plucked your eyebrows just a little too much, resulting in a look of permanent surprise? Even when you smile and pose prettily before the camera, you still look as if you are questioning the whole process.

Your eyebrows will grow back, but likely not in time for your Facebook photo to be taken.

Quick Fix:

Create filled in brows that are less of a surprise with your eye pencil. If your eyebrows are dark, use a pencil that is a shade lighter. If they are light, use a pencil that is a shade darker.

Gently stroke color into the sparse areas to change your look. Draw in new brows where you need them. Do not do what your women in your grandmother's era did, which was just draw a line on the eyebrow.

That gives you an artificial look. The gentle shading will give you the fill in that you need without creating another makeup faux pas.

Once your eyebrows grow in, get a professional to reshape them and then your job will just be to maintain the look.

You look like Halloween came early

You decided to be adventurous and try some of those new hot pink and green mascara shades on the market. Somewhere you also read that it was a good idea to give yourself two or three mascara applications before having your picture taken.

Now when you look at your eyes, you get an unworldly feeling, like a strange-colored spider is perched above your eyes, just ready to pounce down on the rest of your face.

Quick Fix:

If you have a spare pair of false eyelashes, you just might want to put them on now.

Even that might not do the trick. Instead, holding a paper towel below your eyelashes, gently use a cotton swap dipped in eye makeup remover to get the bulk of the mascara off.

Once your lashes have dried, reapply just one coat of mascara. Keep in mind that if your complexion and your hair are darker, use black mascara. Brown mascara or even black/brown colors work well with lighter lashes.

Don't throw out your fun colors. Save them for an evening out when you aren't planning to pose for a photo, and just settle for one application.

You are underwhelmed by your features

In doing your makeup for your Facebook photo, you spend considerable time on your eyes, your lips, your cheekbones and even concealing your flaws. But someone the face that stares back at you is under-whelming.

There is no one feature that dominates your face and draws people to you. Instead, while you look "all right" you do not look "wow." It is disheartening after all the effort you put into it.

What has happened is that in your effort to bring out the best in your features, you forget to select one to dominate your look. Since everything is done well, nothing looks distinctive enough to capture another person's attention.

Quick Fix:

As a general rule, the features that will most likely dominate your face are your eyes and your lips. Do what the Duchess of Cambridge Kate Middleton does. Her rule is always to focus on either eyes or lips, never both.

If she selects the eyes as the feature in focus, she uses lots of liquid eyeliner and mascara. If the focus is on lips, she selects a lip gloss darker than what she normally wears.

You also need to decide which feature you want to take the spotlight.

If it is your eyes, tone down your lips a little. Bring your lip color down a notch and a little closer to your natural shade.

If you want to focus on your lips, tone down your eyes a little. Soften the liner a bit and tone down the shadow to be closer to your natural skin tone.

You look like Cleopatra

You did your best to create drama around your eyes, but when you look quickly at the mirror just before you pose for your Facebook photo, you realize you should really be leaving for a boat trip down the Nile.

If your eyeliner has turned you into Cleopatra, it is likely you have overdone it.

Quick Fix:

The overly-dramatic Cleopatra eye is created when you extend your liquid eye liner far beyond the end of the eye and sweep it into an upwards curve.

Just be dabbing a bit of translucent powder on it and gently brushing out the extended line, you can solve the problem.

As a general rule, if you are not used to applying liquid eyeliner, start by applying a thin line from the inner corner of your eye to the outer corner and stop. If it is not sufficiently dramatic, add a second narrow line this time gently blending up from the middle of the eye to the outer corner.

So go and get your Facebook photo done. If you discover more than one makeup look that you love, you may end up changing your profile photo more than once!